British Railways Pictorial

Railways of Kent

Anthony W. Burges

First published 2007

ISBN (10) 0 7110 3165 7
ISBN (13) 978 0 7110 3165 4

© Anthony W. Burges 2007

Published by Ian Allan Publishing

an imprint of Ian Allan Publishing Ltd,
Hersham, Surrey KT12 4RG.
Printed in England by Ian Allan Printing Ltd,
Hersham, Surrey KT12 4RG.

Code: 0702/B

Visit the Ian Allan Publishing website at
www.ianallanpublishing.com

*All photographs by Anthony W. Burges
unless otherwise credited*

This book is dedicated to George Marsh
and Dennis Weaver for years of tolerance
and hospitality at Chestfield & Swalecliffe
Halt in the 1950s.

Front cover: Ex-SECR Class C 0-6-0
No 31481 at Shepherdswell, 23 March 1959.
T. B. Owen

Back cover, top: Ex-SECR Class H 0-4-4T
No 31518 at Chevening Halt, 28 October
1961 on the 14.23 from Westerham.
Colour-Rail

Back cover, middle: 'Schools' class 4-4-0
No 30915 *Brighton* at Folkestone Warren,
April 1960. *Colour-Rail / BRS1587*

Back cover, bottom: BR Standard
Class 2-6-4T No 80087 at New Romney,
4 June 1960. *Colour-Rail / BRS176*

Title page: After crossing the Medway bridge
at Rochester, up Kent coast trains were
confronted with a sharp curve before
grappling with five miles of hard slog up
the 1:100 gradient of Sole Street bank,
which lifted the former LCDR main line
out of the Medway Valley on to the chalk
uplands forming part of the backbone of Kent.
In August 1957, the solid exhaust beat
of 'King Arthur' class 4-6-0 No 30767
Sir Valence with a Ramsgate–Victoria train
could be heard miles away in the valley
below. Time was running out for *Sir Valence*,
one of the 'Scotch Arthurs', built by the
North British Locomotive Company in 1925,
as it was to be withdrawn from service
in 1959. *G. R. Siviour*

CONTENTS

INTRODUCTION

Kent exemplifies the demographic changes that have transformed the Southeast of England in recent years. A few select comparisons demonstrate the evolution of the county from the popular perception of it as the garden of England in the 1950s to something more appropriately described as the dormitory of the Southeast in the early 21st century. County boundaries have been subject to periodic adjustment, with the result that the area of Kent was reduced by 5.5 per cent in 1974 as London grew in size. In the pages that follow, the pre-1974 boundaries have been retained to facilitate comparisons between 1950 and the present day. Thus the population of the old county is now approximately 2 million, a growth of 25 per cent since 1951. In overall terms, Kent is approaching Belgium in population density.

As far as its economic and social linkages were concerned a surprisingly large proportion of the county remained rural and semi-rural in the Fifties. This is no longer the case. Not only has Kent been effectively absorbed into the wider commuter hinterland of London, it is also being increasingly internationalised as a result of the ease of access to the Continent provided by the Channel Tunnel. In another trend, urban development has continued to expand most noticeably along the southern side of the Thames estuary (generally referred to as North Kent), throughout the M25 motorway zone and on the Isle of Thanet.

Many traditional agricultural pursuits that generated important traffic for the railways are now less noticeable. For example, Kent has been eclipsed by Herefordshire as Britain's major hop producer, and fruit from Kentish orchards now faces increasing global competition in the UK market. Transformation in the industrial sector has been equally evident. On the one hand the East Kent coalfield is now little more than a receding memory, while the Isle of Grain has shared in the industrial and port expansion along the Thames estuary.

Concurrently, ongoing service sector and high-tech employment expansion is now widely dispersed throughout the county. Seaside resorts that owed their growth and prosperity to the arrival of the railway in the 19th century have adapted to new roles as residences for increasing numbers of commuters and retirees, while attracting car-borne day trippers rather than long-stay visitors. The consolidation of port facilities brought about by technological change such as containerisation has supported the growth of Thamesport on the Isle of Grain, although Dover is still a major port for car and truck orientated ferry traffic and has become a focal point for the cruise ship business favoured by today's prosperous society.

Elsewhere, railways have ceased to play a role at smaller ports such as Gravesend, Whitstable, Faversham Creek, Ramsgate, Richborough and Folkestone, and the county has increasingly become a transit zone for long-haul rail and road freight which originates at or is destined for points beyond its borders both at home and overseas. The long-established defence sector has declined and many facilities have been put to new uses, examples being Chatham Dockyard, now a tourist attraction, and Manston in the civil aviation sector. Motorways encircle London and link it to the Channel Tunnel and ferry terminals. Ever-increasing levels of car ownership have made the countryside easily accessible while creating increased congestion and contributing to a steady rise in property values.

As in Hampshire, the vital role of the railways is well understood and, not surprisingly, the rail network has not only survived these changes largely intact, but is now almost entirely electrified. The progression of railway electrification is depicted by map on page 8. In 1950, the total rail route mileage within the county was 450½. Since then, a limited number of abandonments have been offset by the opening of the first section of the Channel Tunnel Rail Link (CTRL) from Fawkham Junction to Dollands Moor. As a result, the route mileage (using pre-1974 boundaries) was 439 in 2005. The CTRL (the first truly high-speed line in Britain) was primarily designed to meet the needs of London and Europe, although Kentish commuters will derive some benefits from it in the near future.

In the Fifties, the railways of Kent were poised on the threshold of major changes. These included the end of steam traction and the virtual completion of electrification, the loss of traditional seasonal holiday business, the transfer of most non-bulk freight to road transport, and expansion in commuting by rail. In an era where branch line and station closures were to become a common feature in the evolution of the rail network of southern England, Kent was to emerge relatively unscathed with only 71¼ miles being closed to all traffic. These line closures resulted in the loss of 42 stations, with a further ten stations disappearing elsewhere on the network, as well as three on the 15-inch gauge Romney, Hythe & Dymchurch Railway.

The most notable loss has been the imposing Dover Western Docks (formerly Dover Marine) terminus, whose role was made redundant when the Channel Tunnel opened in 1994. The maps on pages 4 and 12 illustrate the very limited adjustments to the railway map of Kent. Potentially, there is a vast agenda to be addressed here and it is therefore essential at the outset to define the focus as one which concentrates on steam rather than electric traction, and primarily relates to that part of Kent which lies beyond the suburbs of London. The time frame encompasses the second half of the 20th century plus the years following the millennium, but with an emphasis on the 1950s.

A personal context

For the author, Kent was a special place. Visits to a grandmother who lived at Swalecliffe meant some respite from war-torn London in the school holidays and the bliss of two-hour journeys on steam trains. Notwithstanding the proximity of East Kent to enemy-occupied France, the area was relatively safe, with the exception of the shoreline around Dover which was within artillery range of the French coast.

A great delight was the commanding view from my summer home of the Victoria–Ramsgate main line along which there was a daily parade of vintage motive power, often seen hauling hastily repaired rolling stock. Among the vignettes etched in my memory was a spectacular sight one night of a 'C' class 0-6-0 on a goods which had sustained a blowback, with the footplate crew hanging on for dear life and doubtless hoping that the guard would notice the conflagration and apply the brakes. However, my very earliest memory of Kent was that of riding a chocolate and yellow tram on the three-quarter-mile length of Herne Bay Pier, just before war broke out.

My association with Swalecliffe continued up until the mid-1950s. By that time I had spent many summers as a member of the 'railway children' and regularly assisted the friendly staff at Chestfield & Swalecliffe Halt with many duties. Most importantly, I was able to witness, at first hand, the postwar boom in holiday traffic which was to be the last hurrah of steam traction – a subject to which I will return later. Among other joys was the occasional cycle ride to Blean Woods, or the site of

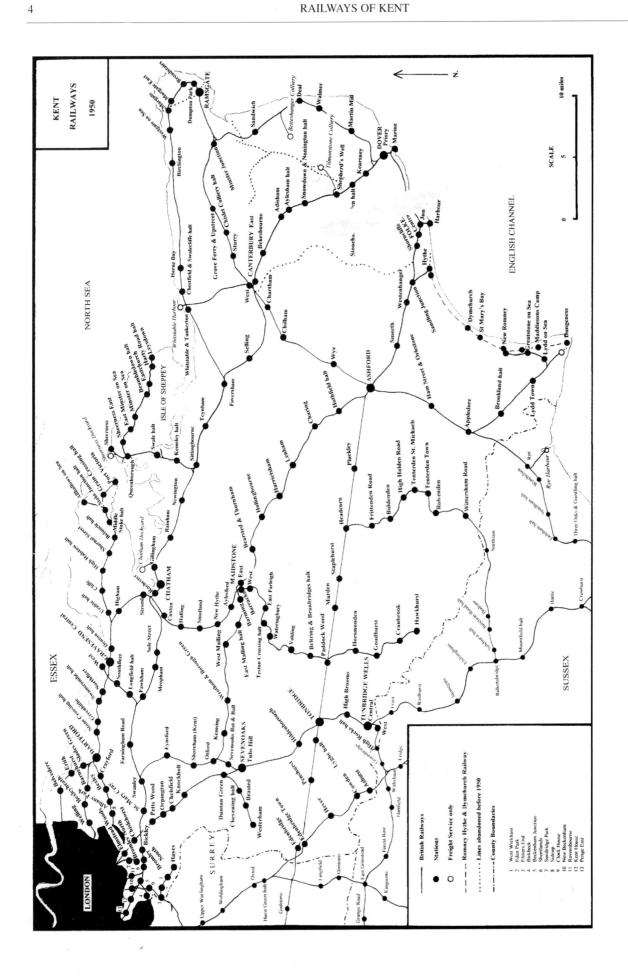

South Street Halt to see the passing of the daily Canterbury West–Whitstable Harbour goods train on Kent's oldest railway.

Another treasured memory was the sight from an East Kent bus, held at the level crossing on the Deal–Canterbury route, of a grimy 'O1' fly shunting a solitary coach and an assortment of wagons on the East Kent Light Railway at Canterbury Road, Wingham. From the beach at Swalecliffe the prominent headland of Shell Ness at the eastern tip of the Isle of Sheppey was for many years, both intriguing and unattainable. Thus, when my first branch line journey took place in 1950, it was on the late-lamented Sheppey Light Railway between Queenborough and Leysdown. Unfortunately, I did not possess a camera at the time. In any event these experiences set me on a lifelong quest for railway backwaters and a career which involved me deeply in branch line issues in three countries.

Main lines in a troubled era

It was obvious from the station architecture, consisting generally of modest weatherboard or brick structures inherited from the companies who built the rail system of Kent, that the early railways did not possess deep pockets and even the later veneer of Southern Railway concrete could not disguise that fact. Nicknames such as the 'London Smash 'em and Over' for the London, Chatham & Dover Railway and the 'Slow, Easy and Comfortable' for the South Eastern & Chatham Railway, amusing though seldom fully justified, implied very limited expectations on the part of the public. These attitudes lived on through the Fifties.

The complex railway history of the county has been addressed comprehensively and well by others, and space limitations do not permit revisiting it in what is essentially a pictorial survey. Nonetheless, in 1950, it was clear that the railway network still bore the stamp of the pre-Grouping companies: the South Eastern, the London, Chatham & Dover, and the product of their subsequent union, the South Eastern & Chatham. The western margin of the county was barely touched by the London, Brighton & South Coast Railway. In spite of the spread of Southern Railway standardisation, the system still bore the scars of the damage and lack of investment attributable to World War II.

The topographic barrier represented by the chalk ridge of the North Downs was an important factor in both the selection of routes and the construction costs incurred

as main lines extended from London to the channel ports and the Kent coast. The early South Eastern Railway route to Dover via Redhill and Tonbridge was circuitous and subsequent competition necessitated the construction of a cut-off route via Chislehurst and Sevenoaks to Tonbridge. This conquered the North Downs by means of the Chelsfield, Polhill and Sevenoaks tunnels, while the rival London, Chatham & Dover faced similar tunnelling challenges within the Medway towns and on the route from Faversham to Dover. In fact, tunnels have always been notable features of Kent's railways.

Plans for main line electrification were cut short in 1939 by the advent of World War II, so that main line passenger services remained largely in the hands of 'King Arthur' 4-6-0s, 'Schools' 4-4-0s and a wide variety of older 4-4-0s of 'D', 'E', and 'L' classes and their rebuilt versions, 'D1' and 'E1'. Moguls of 'N' and 'N1' classes were mainstays of both local passenger and goods services which also relied heavily too on 0-6-0s drawn from 'C', 'Q' and the later 'Q1' classes. Modernisation was slowly becoming evident by the early 1950s with the appearance of Bulleid light Pacifics of the 'West Country'/'Battle of Britain' class,

RAIL LINE CLOSURES IN KENT 1950–2005

Section	Mileage	No of stations closed (P)	Date
Queenborough–Leysdown (Sheppey Light Rly)	8.75	7	4/12/50
Grain–Port Victoria	1.00	1	11/6/51
Sandling Junction–Hythe	1.50	1	3/12/51
Canterbury West–Whitstable Harbour	6.00		1/12/52
Fawkham Junction–Gravesend West (P)	4.75	3	3/8/53
Headcorn–Tenterden Town (former KESR)	8.00	4	4/12/54
Tenterden Town–Sussex border (A) (former KESR)	5.50	3	12/6/61
Paddock Wood–Hawkhurst	11.50	4	12/6/61
Dunton Green–Westerham	4.75	3	30/10/61
Hoo Junction–Grain (P)	10.00	8	4/12/61
Stoke Junction–Allhallows-on-Sea	1.75	1	4/12/61
Faversham Creek branch	1.25		1964
Appledore–Lydd Town (P)	7.00	2	6/3/67
Lydd Town–New Romney	6.50	3	6/3/67
Fawkham Junction–Gravesend West* (B)	4.75		24/3/68
Shepherds Well–Tilmanstone Colliery (A)	2.75		1/3/84
Grove Junction–Sussex border (A) (Eridge to Tunbridge Wells West branch)	1.75	2	6/12/85
Betteshanger Colliery branch	2.00		1989

(A) Subsequently became part of a heritage railway.
(B) Subsequently a portion of this line became part of the Channel Tunnel Rail Link.
(P) Closed to passenger traffic; all other lines listed were closed to all traffic.
* Coal trains to APCM (Blue Circle) continued until 1976.

OTHER STATION CLOSURES IN KENT 1950–2005

Station	Closed
High Rocks Halt	1952
Margate East	1953
Smeeth	1954
Stonehall & Lydden Halt	1954
Hothfield Halt	1959
Teston Crossing Halt	1959
Denton Halt	1961
Grove Ferry	1966
Chislet Halt	1971
Greatstone-on-Sea (RHDR)	c1975
Lade Halt (RHDR)	c1975
Pilot Halt (RHDR)	c1975
Dover Western Docks (Marine)	1994

while the heavier 'Merchant Navy' Pacifics were often assigned to top-link express workings such as the 'Golden Arrow'. Later in the decade, new BR Standard 4-6-0s and 2-6-4Ts were making their appearance throughout the Southern Region.

The rapidly ageing stock of life-expired motive power was complemented by a pool of passenger coaches that dated back to the 19th century. It was still commonplace to encounter ex-SECR carriages on main line services, and what a delight it

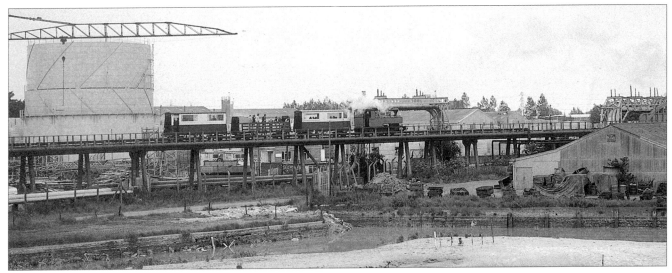

was to recline amidst the faded Victorian splendour of the first class saloon section of a 'birdcage' set, but Maunsell corridor stock was the norm. The problem was that after years of wartime austerity and deprivation, the travel demands of the public, particularly where holidays were concerned, were burgeoning in a society where car ownership remained the exception rather than the rule.

My experiences at Chestfield & Swalecliffe Halt represented a microcosm of an exhausted railway that was under siege. Swalecliffe was then a community of mainly retired people and possessed extensive shingle beaches and shoreline marshland supporting large caravan and camping sites. Chestfield reflected another part of the social spectrum in which commuting to London was more popular. Thus holidaymakers and commuters were the principal rail users at this unprepossessing halt. The inconvenient locations of the stations serving the neighbouring towns of Whitstable and Herne Bay meant that local travel was largely the monopoly of the stately Dennis Lancet single-decker buses of the curiously named East Kent Road Car Company.

There were a surprisingly large number of London commuters on the Kent coast, and Chestfield & Swalecliffe Halt alone generated some 110 daily travellers to Cannon Street, of whom a significant proportion travelled first class. Interestingly, the fastest business services covered the 59 miles from Whitstable to Cannon Street in 70 minutes. This required some spirited assaults on Sole Street bank and the Bulleid Pacifics performed well on these ten-coach trains. Today, notwithstanding the undoubted benefits of electrification, performance has tended to regress

and such timings are seldom equalled, let alone surpassed. Summer Saturdays were particularly exciting and saw the Ramsgate line working to capacity. Large numbers of caravanners and campers arrived from London and stations on the north Kent line. Every available locomotive was drafted into service to haul trains often crammed with standing passengers.

Through trains from Woolwich Arsenal, Erith and other North Kent line stations frequently consisted of eight-coach 'birdcage' sets. After a two-hour journey in vintage non-corridor stock and arriving at a station which possessed none of the usual conveniences, the agony of many passengers was palpable, with results which did not endear them to the villagers. Late running was commonplace and one could often see the steam and smoke of a line of up trains held at signals far away to the east.

Loco crews sometimes misread their special traffic notices, with the result that trains that were supposed to stop at Chestfield went sailing through while others that were not scheduled to stop did so. On one disastrous Saturday a through train bound for Sheffield made an unauthorised stop, and with several hundred people on the platform it was impossible to prevent passengers from boarding. It was apparent that nobody was puzzled by the sight of varnished-teak Gresley rolling stock of the former LNER. As its next timetabled stop after Whitstable was Woodford Halse on the old Great Central main line, one had visions of bewildered Londoners unexpectedly finding themselves in rural Northamptonshire.

On another occasion, the failure of a 'D' class 4-4-0 halfway between Whitstable and Chestfield resulted in the casualty and its train being propelled into Chestfield by

Above: The Sittingbourne & Kemsley Light Railway derives from a 2ft 6in-gauge industrial line owned by Bowaters to carry raw materials between this paper company's two mills. After closure the line was offered to the Locomotive Club of Great Britain, heritage services commencing in 1969. On 15 June 1975, Bagnall 0-6-2T *Triumph* crosses Sittingbourne viaduct, the first and longest reinforced-concrete viaduct in the world, with a Kemsley Down train.

the following train which was mercifully in the capable hands of a 'Schools' class 4-4-0. It took several hours to unscramble the ensuing chaos, with trains backed up all along the line as far away as Sittingbourne. There was also the immediate challenge of shepherding passengers who had jumped down on to the track from the crippled train beyond the end of the down platform before a disaster occurred.

Campers and caravanners tended to bring everything but the kitchen sink with them and the writer narrowly avoided being buried by an avalanche of luggage when opening the doors of a 'birdcage' brake compartment on a particularly frantic Saturday. The guard was not notably sympathetic and the delay was considerable. Memories such as these indicate the impossible pressures that were then being placed on a run-down railway, although recent cross-country journeys in Britain conveyed a certain sense of *déjà vu*!

Notwithstanding the fact that the LCDR had targeted Dover in its early days, the route from Faversham to Dover was much quieter than the coastal section to Ramsgate. Prior to electrification, it offered a pleasant and fairly unhurried rural ride and most services stopped at all stations. Much of the local traffic had already been captured by the network of

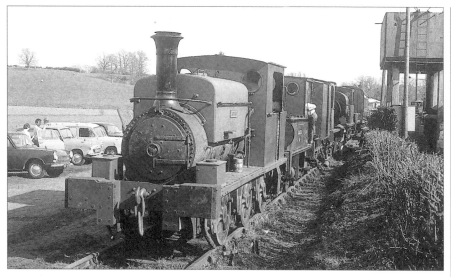

Left: The Kent & East Sussex Railway of Colonel Holman F. Stephens operated passenger services through the Rother Valley from 1900 to 1954, after which freight traffic continued until 1961. Subsequent efforts by preservationists to reopen the line have been successful, heritage services thriving today between Bodiam and Tenterden Town.
In August 1968 four locomotives are displayed at Rolvenden, with Manning Wardle 0-6-0ST No 17 *Arthur* in the foreground.

East Kent bus services that radiated out from Canterbury. The Dover line carried the output of Snowdown Colliery, where some sidings were provided with catenary for shunting purposes following electrification, as well as coal from Tilmanstone Colliery via a connection at Shepherds Well. The line provided one of three possible routes to London for Dover boat trains prior to the advent of the CTRL, although the steeper grades of the LCDR route were a disadvantage.

The former SER main line to Dover comprised four distinctly different operating environments. On leaving Charing Cross trains had to contend with the congestion and complexity of the suburban electrified area before the chalk barrier of the North Downs was conquered by tunnels at Chelsfield, Polhill and Sevenoaks en route to Tonbridge. Thereafter, the job of loco crews was eased by the long straight and level section of the Wealden racetrack to Ashford, where the station was later to be upgraded to 'international' status with the opening of the Channel Tunnel. The final challenge was that of the geologically unstable coastal route between Folkestone and Dover.

Extensions from Ashford to Minster via Canterbury West and from Dover to Ramsgate via Deal were relatively quiet in spite of the coal traffic from Chislet and Betteshanger collieries. Weekend holiday traffic to resorts such as Folkestone was intense and London commuting patterns were already well established at many country stations such as Headcorn and Paddock Wood. Continental goods traffic to and from Dover was heavy, and the 'Night Ferry' with its dark blue Wagons Lits sleeping cars added a touch of exotica. The line also handled some of the now-forgotten seasonal passenger trains serving hop-pickers and hop-pickers' friends which gave veteran steam power and rolling stock an occasional outing. The scenic Hastings main line south of Tonbridge carried its fair share of London commuters and seasonal holidaymakers, together with a flow of gypsum from the mine at Mountfield.

With the spread of electrification and the dieselisation of other lines, a familiar feature of the railway scene in Kent, the final steam locomotive sheds, vanished quite rapidly from the mid-1950s.

The last days of steam loco sheds in Kent

Historical records indicate the existence of an additional 17 sheds in earlier days, but the numbers declined as a result of the rationalisation attributable to the formation of the South Eastern & Chatham Railway Management Committee in 1899, electrification which began in 1926, line closures, and the demise of the light railways managed by Colonel Stephens. The large railway works at Ashford, which was built by the South Eastern Railway in 1845, ceased operation in 1982, during which time nearly one thousand locomotives had been built or rebuilt there, as well as the manufacture and servicing of rolling stock.

Secondary routes

Several secondary routes have retained a particular significance. These include the busy suburban commuter lines which converge upon Dartford. Of these the North Kent line still generates significant goods traffic in which the yard at Hoo Junction plays a strategic role. The Medway Valley line from Strood to Maidstone West and Paddock Wood continues to serve industrial activities at its northern end, while south of Maidstone it provides an important link to Redhill and beyond for freight traffic as well as a local passenger service between Maidstone and Gatwick Airport. A suggestion that occasionally surfaces is the proposal to utilise the Strood to Maidstone section as a route for a Medway Valley light rail system, although current prospects for such a development remain dim.

The Redhill–Paddock Wood section has featured in the long-distance freight route advocated by the Central Railway. The line

THE FINAL STEAM LOCOMOTIVE SHEDS IN KENT (1900–1964)

Location	Opening date	Closure date	Shed codes, from 1950
Ashford	1931	1963 (steam) 1968 (diesel)	74A, 73F (from 10/58)
Canterbury West	1846	1955	subshed to 74A
Dover Marine	1928	1961	74C, 73H (10/58)
Faversham	1860	1959	73E
Folkestone Junction	1899	1961	subshed to 74C, subshed to 73H (10/58)
Gillingham	1885	1960	73D, 73J (6/59)
Ramsgate	1930	1959	74B, 73G (10/58), 73F (06/59)
Rolvenden	1900	1954	subshed to 74A
Tonbridge	1842	1962	74D, 75D (1962)
Tunbridge Wells West	1890	1963	75F

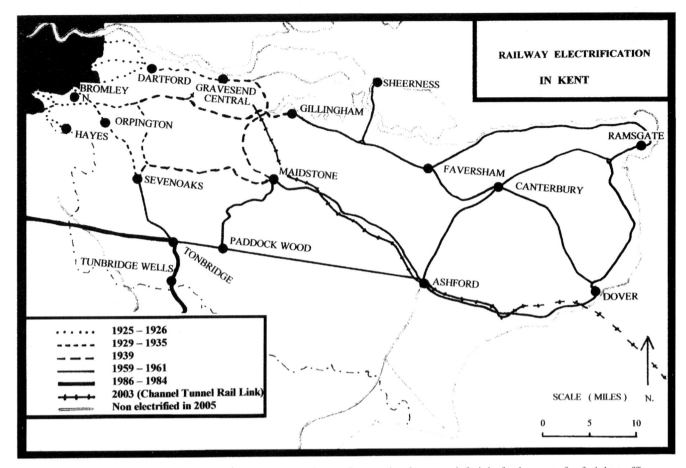

RAILWAY ELECTRIFICATION

IN KENT

from Swanley through Otford to Maidstone East and along the foot of the North Downs to Ashford, formerly of diversionary value for boat trains and freight, has evolved into a mainly commuter route. Interestingly, it now forms part of a transport corridor with the Channel Tunnel Rail Link and the M20 motorway from east of Hollingbourne to the edge of the Ashford urban area. Several of its intermediate stations east of Maidstone currently generate very limited passenger traffic and have been identified as possible candidates for service cutbacks, the line having lost much of its former significance as a diversionary route. Uncertainty also hovers over some of the quieter stations on the Medway Valley line.

Branch lines with a future

Two lines penetrating the low-lying terrain bounded by the Thames and Medway estuaries deserve a mention because they serve areas of existing or potential importance for the rail network of Kent. The Hundred of Hoo branch from Hoo Junction Yard to the Isle of Grain industrial zone has had a somewhat chequered history in which the varying fortunes of the cement industry, oil refining, uralite manufacture and defence installations have played a role, while power generation and port development are more recent growth factors. At one time the branch was a strategic element in competition between the SER and the LCDR for European ferry services and as a route for the SER to challenge the LCDR monopoly on the Isle of Sheppey, via the ill-fated terminal at Port Victoria.

The Hundred of Hoo was also a magnet for visionaries intent on developing Allhallows-on-Sea as a residential site and holiday resort. The author remembers well the litany of halts announced on the public address system at Gravesend Central station prior to the departure of an 'H' class 0-4-4T and its poorly patronised two-coach train which seemed strangely out of place amongst the electric multiple-units that thronged the North Kent line. For the enthusiast venturing out into the Hundred of Hoo in the Fifties the somewhat faded classic SER weatherboard stations at Cliffe and Sharnal Street were interspersed by stark, concrete halts in treeless locations before arrival at the terminus at Allhallows. There, the typical Southern station architecture of the 1930s seemed to be an anomaly in such a deserted place. Undoubtedly, the line to Grain had a distinctive character, but it has perhaps come into its own in its current role as a

freight feeder route for freight traffic.

The branch from Sittingbourne to Sheerness has a history similar to that of the Hundred of Hoo line in terms of fluctuations in the past role of the ports it served at Sheerness and Queenborough Pier, the decline of Sheerness dockyard and the survival of the Settle Speakman spur at Queenborough. The recent reopening of the rail connection to Ridham Dock, near Swale Halt, has restored some freight traffic. The impact on the surviving electrified branch passenger service of the new high-level highway bridge connecting Sheppey to the mainland is unpredictable, but the closure of Swale Halt appears to be an imminent possibility.

The third branch line survivor continues to function because it performs a special role dictated by government regulations which require the conveyance of nuclear waste to be handled by rail. Thus the spur linking the Dungeness nuclear generating station to the Ashford–Hastings line at Appledore is a strategic, if truncated, portion of the former New Romney branch. It is likely to continue performing its highly specialised role of moving flasks of nuclear waste for processing at Sellafield for as long as the power station is in operation.

Branch lines with a past

By contrast, there were a number of railway byways for which the writing was clearly on the wall in the years between 1950 and 1990. The factors contributing to their demise varied considerably, from the irretrievable loss of passengers and goods to road competition, lack of relevance to local travel patterns, operating restrictions that impeded goods traffic, the disappearance of established industries that were the principal source of traffic and the opening of the Channel Tunnel.

Road competition

The Sheppey Light Railway (closed 4 December 1950), which ran from Queenborough to Leysdown, was a casualty because it served a thinly populated area of the island that was devoid of industry and terminated at a small resort which scarcely met the expectations of its promoters. In true light railway style, the progress of each of the four weekdays-only trains was slow due to the number of unstaffed level crossings that had to be opened and closed for the passage of each train by the guard. Vintage steam in the form of 'R' class 0-4-4Ts hauling a converted articulated SECR steam railcar set further condemned the line to a 'connoisseur' category beloved by railway enthusiasts, but shunned by most other travellers who took the Maidstone & District bus service to Sheerness. The Leysdown shoreline was noteworthy for its eclectic array of pre-Grouping coach bodies that provided accommodation for visitors.

The truncated remnant of the Sandgate branch offered a derisory service linking Sandling Junction to Hythe where the station was poorly situated in relation to the town centre. A local bus operator provided a more frequent and convenient service. The decline in public awareness of the existence of the line was evident when a random street survey by the author revealed that most citizens understood that the Romney, Hythe & Dymchurch establishment was the only station in Hythe, although a number of respondents insisted either that there had not been a train service from the Southern station for years, or that the station did not exist. Even an attempt to convince the booking clerk at Ashford that it was still possible to reach Hythe by train resulted in a lengthy argument! The end came on 3 December 1951, and this was to be the first of a large number of 'funerals' attended by the author during the pre-Beeching era.

The Kent & East Sussex line from Headcorn to Robertsbridge was a mecca for pilgrims intent on enjoying the delights of this survivor of the scattered light railway empire of Colonel Stephens. Unfortunately, its vestigial goods traffic, low speed and the infrequency of its trains rendered it of little value to commuters, the general public and local businesses in spite of its main line connections. It is perhaps ironic to note that the antique features of the line that led to its demise were to become the very same attractions that subsequently assured its partial rebirth and well-deserved success as a preserved heritage railway.

The Paddock Wood–Hawkhurst branch was long treasured as the archetypal Kentish railway backwater. It remained steam-worked until the end came in 1961 and followed what seemed to be a somewhat uncertain path through rolling farmland, dotted with hop gardens and oast houses. Convenience to the passenger was never its strong card since Goudhurst station was separated from its village by an intimidating hill, while both Cranbrook and Hawkhurst stations were taxi journeys or long walks from the communities they purported to serve. For the hop pickers from southeast London who arrived in special trains the line must have seemed like a route to the back of beyond. If it had survived longer it might well have become

Below: What is now known as the Marshlink line between Ashford and Hastings is one of the few lines in south-east England never to have been electrified. Traffic levels necessitated the augmentation of the capacity of DEMUs on this service, producing aberrations which were christened 'Tadpoles'. In August 1987 No 206101 leaves Ham Street station, formerly known as Ham Street & Orlestone.

a prime candidate for preservation. Instead, its memory recalls a vanished age when branch lines performed a valued, if unprofitable, function in rural areas. The main line stations at Staplehurst, Marden, Paddock Wood and Tunbridge Wells Central had become the preferred railheads for the area served by the branch long before it was abandoned.

The scenic Westerham Valley line, in spite of its closer proximity to London and its use by commuters who connected at Dunton Green with outer suburban electric services, competed with the faster and more frequent services available at Sevenoaks (Tubs Hill) and Oxted. Its closure in 1961 was controversial and a further heritage railway opportunity was attempted, but was lost as for most of its length, it suffered the ultimate indignity of being literally buried by the M25 motorway.

Decreasing relevance to local travel patterns
In the early 1950s, the former LCDR branch from Farningham Road (which left the main line at Fawkham Junction) to Gravesend West Street was an oasis of pure steam in the electrified area. Infrequent two-coach push-pull trains powered by Kirtley 'R1' 0-4-4Ts served sadly neglected stations, although the somewhat cramped goods facilities at Gravesend West remained important because of the lack of space at Gravesend Central. It was obvious in 1953 that closure was inevitable since the main passenger flows to and from London were concentrated on the regular-interval electric services that served Gravesend Central on the North Kent line, and Farningham Road and Fawkham on the former LCDR main line.

Freight services lingered for a further 15 years and the line then seemed destined to fade from the landscape. Instead, and in contrast to the fate of the Westerham Valley line, a major section of the branch, from Fawkham Junction to a point near the site of Southfleet station was subsequently incorporated into Stage 1 of the Channel Tunnel Rail Link. So here was a unique situation for Kent in which a decaying branch line was closed, consigned to a period of dereliction and then resurrected as a component of a new high-speed line. Perhaps there are further surprises to come as the future of the Fawkham Junction–Southfleet section once again becomes doubtful with the completion of Stage 2 of the CTRL in 2007.

Another instance of inconvenience for travellers was the circuitous nature of main line access and the infrequency of service for passengers on the New Romney branch, often requiring a change of train at both Appledore and Ashford. Direct bus services to Ashford finally triumphed, leaving just a truncated spur carrying nuclear waste from Dungeness power station.

The impediment of operating restrictions
Notwithstanding its historical significance, the line linking Canterbury West to Whitstable Harbour suffered because of its age. By 1950, motive power was restricted to ancient 'R' class 0-6-0Ts with cut-down cabs and shortened chimneys that could operate through the half-mile length of Tyler Hill Tunnel. There was no passenger rolling stock that could be used on the line, although this had ceased to be a concern since 1931, and there were also tunnel-related loading gauge limitations that inhibited freight traffic. Even the grain wagons that formed a significant part of the goods traffic required special modification. Closure of the 'Crab and Winkle' line was inevitable in 1952, although it is regrettable that the opportunity to convert the line into a heritage trail was not seized. If abandonment had occurred towards the end of the 20th century the response would almost certainly have been very different.

Loss of industrial traffic base
The East Kent coalfield was a relatively short-lived chapter in the history of Britain's mining industry. Following a number of abortive ventures at Shakespeare Cliff, Wingham, Guilford and Stonehall, working collieries were finally established at four locations. Each was served by rail, with branch lines or sidings connected to a main line. The first mine to commence operation was at Snowdown in 1912, followed by Tilmanstone in 1913. Chislet came on stream in 1918, and Betteshanger was the last to open, in 1927.

The mining villages which sprang up at Aylesham, Hersden and Elvington were quite unlike other Kentish communities. Chislet ceased operations due to geological problems in 1969, followed by Snowdown and Tilmanstone in 1987, and finally by Betteshanger in 1989. The rump of the former East Kent Light Railway which served Tilmanstone and a two-mile spur linking Betteshanger to the Dover-Deal line were inevitable casualties, although a portion of the former has been transformed into a heritage railway.

Impact of the Channel Tunnel
The short spur connecting Dover Western Docks (formerly Dover Marine) station with the main line was no longer required with the opening of Dollands Moor Yard and the commencement of the shuttle, passenger and goods services through the Channel Tunnel to Fréthun in 1994. This resulted in the loss of one of Kent's most impressive stations.

Ruins and resurrection
As viewed from the air, Kent exhibits fewer traces of abandoned railways than most English counties. Perhaps the most notable scar on the landscape is that of the Elham Valley line from Harbledown Junction Canterbury to Cheriton Junction west of Shorncliffe, which was finally closed in 1947 after a military takeover during World War II. Following the Elham Valley and penetrating the chalk upland of the North Downs by means of the Bourne and Etchinghill tunnels, the line was never busy. It was built to deter the LCDR from venturing into the SER's Folkestone market. Four of the original six stations survive, at Lyminge, Bishopsbourne, Bridge and Canterbury South. Given the attractive scenery through which it passed, it is regrettable that closure occurred long before the advent of Sustrans, when abandoned railway rights of way were not regarded as candidates for conversion to hiking and cycle paths.

Because of their limited earthworks the abandoned light railways of Kent have tended to vanish quite quickly as old roadbeds have reverted to agricultural uses. Thus, only vestigial traces remain of the former Sheppey Light Railway, the East Kent Light Railway from Eythorne to Wingham and the Richborough port area, and the Kent & East Sussex Railway between Headcorn and Tenterden Town. Even the Canterbury & Whitstable line and the delightful byway to Hawkhurst require a discerning eye to detect their remains today.

The good news is that, on the other hand, the railway preservation movement can claim significant successes in Kent with the rebirth of a section of the Kent & East Sussex line from Tenterden Town to Bodiam, the preservation of a short portion of the former East Kent Light Railway connecting Shepherds Well to Eythorne, the restoration of the route from close to Tunbridge Wells West station to (hopefully) Eridge in East Sussex as the Spa Valley Railway, and the continued operation of part of a former narrow gauge industrial line as the Sittingbourne &

Left: Interior view of Dover Western Docks (formerly Dover Marine) on 28 August 1994. After the opening of the Channel Tunnel this cavernous terminus remained in use briefly as a convenient reversal point for electric multiple units employed on the Faversham–Dover service, but finally closed on 25 September 1994. In the foreground is Class 411 '4-CEP' No 1617, with a similar unit arriving on platform 5.

county, but by 1950 only two survivors remained. The Chattenden & Upnor connected naval installations on the lower Medway and ran occasional passenger services for employees. The author was fortunate to travel on this 2ft 6in gauge line behind diesel power before it was closed in 1961. The last remnant of the military railways is now to be found at Lydd on Romney Marsh, where a 2ft gauge system moves personnel and hauls targets on the local gunnery ranges.

The future

Railways have an assured future in Kent and the present passenger network appears to be fairly stable. The CTRL may be expected to handle an ever-growing volume of passenger and freight traffic subject, of course, to the vagaries of regulatory change and the protectionist policies of governments. The imminent prospect of high-speed long-haul Kentish commuter services using Hitachi-built units on the CTRL will test the principle of premium fares for reduced travel time and the viability of St Pancras as a London railhead for increasing numbers of commuters, and may have unforeseeable impacts upon the evolution of the comparatively recently modernised 750V dc network in Kent.

Kemsley Light Railway. Tucked away in a delightful rural setting, a relative newcomer, the private, steam-operated narrow gauge Bredgar & Wormshill Light Railway, situated between Hollingbourne and Sittingbourne, occasionally opens its doors to visitors.

A unique survivor is the mainly tourist-orientated 15-inch gauge Romney, Hythe & Dymchurch Railway, which extends from Hythe to Dungeness and continues to serve a section of coastline bordering Romney Marsh currently undergoing rapid urbanisation. Another curio was the now-closed electrified narrow gauge Ramsgate Tunnel Railway which used part of the original LCDR tunnel to Ramsgate Harbour for part of its length. Billed as a scenic railway, it offered the bemused traveller a series of illuminated tableaux to alleviate the darkness of its subterranean route. When visited in the early 1950s it presented a somewhat faded appearance.

Industrial and military railways

Although these categories of railways are generally beyond the focus of this survey, brief reference to them is justified since they continued to play an important role in the Fifties when industrial railways, many of which were narrow gauge, served the cement industry at Cliffe, Frindsbury, Halling, Northfleet, Sittingbourne,

Snodland and Swanscombe as well as the associated clay and loam sector at Erith and Paddlesworth. The National Coal Board operated small rail systems for shunting purposes at the four collieries comprising the East Kent coalfield, but these ceased operation with the end of mining activities between 1969 and 1989.

Other narrow gauge systems, now abandoned, served the sand and gravel industry near Faversham and at Sturry. The author's first experience of industrial railways in Kent was a tour of the 2ft gauge network operated by the Ace Sand & Gravel Company (subsequently George Brett & Co) on a 'Simplex' diesel locomotive in the area between Faversham and Oare. In addition, there were narrow gauge lines at brickworks located at Murston near Sittingbourne, and at Sandwich. The coal wharves at Rochester were another industrial railway site, and manufacturing activities at Aylesford, Belvedere, Erith, Greenhithe, Kemsley and Northfleet were significant users of private rail systems.

Today road transport has captured most of what remains of this industrial traffic and nearly all these highly individualistic railways have vanished, as have even the industries they served, due to the impact of globalisation.

Historical records indicate the existence of at least 13 military railways within the

Acknowledgements:

Except where stated all photographs are by the author. Special thanks are due to my old friend Gerald Siviour for making available examples of his work which have enriched this survey of the final years of steam in Kent.

I am also indebted to Michael Bowie of Lux Photographic Services of Carleton Place, Ontario for once again breathing new life into my fifty-year-old negatives and to Nick Grant and Matthew Wharmby of Ian Allan Publishing for transforming my text and photographs into what I hope is a most evocative book.

Anthony Burges
Ottawa
January 2007

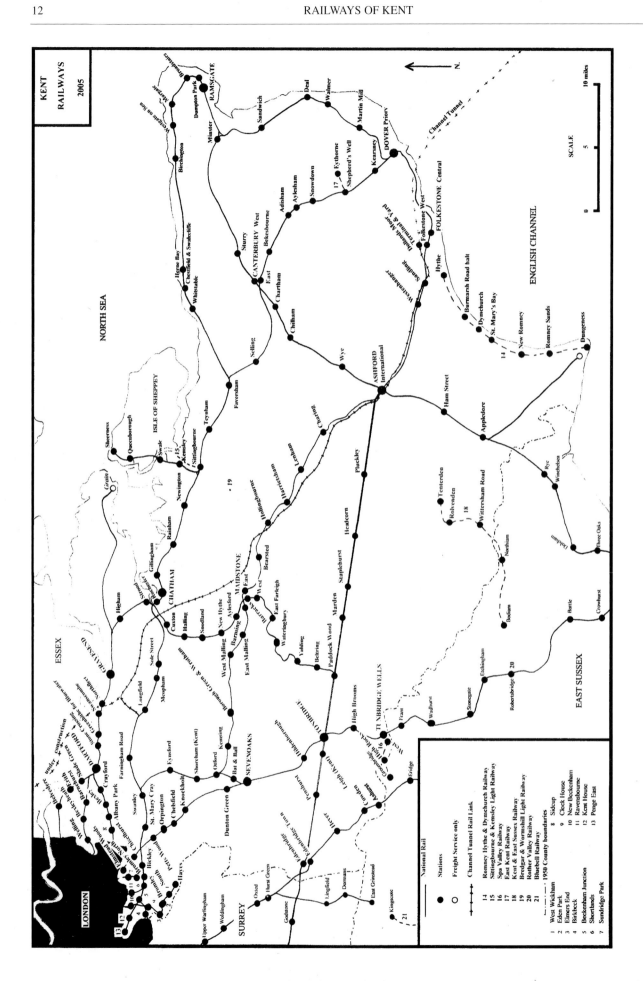

LCDR MAIN LINE VICTORIA–RAMSGATE

Right: The peace of the bucolic country station at Sole Street was frequently disturbed by the passage of steam-hauled expresses en route to and from Ramsgate and Dover. This up train in the capable hands of 'Schools' class 4-4-0 No 30930 *Radley* is accelerating after conquering the notorious Sole Street bank in August 1958. *G. R. Siviour*

Right: Class L1 4-4-0s, built by the North British Locomotive Company in 1925, were regulars on Kent coast trains, and in the hands of accomplished drivers such as Sam Gingell, put in some outstanding performances on Sole Street bank. No 31754 is steaming well with an up train on the long drag in August 1957. Ten of the 15 capable 'L1s' remained in service as late as 1962. *G. R. Siviour*

Below: On the cusp of electrification, in April 1959, a somewhat battered-looking 'L' class 4-4-0 heads for the orchard country east of Gillingham with a local passenger train. *G. R. Siviour*

Right: A 'Schools' class 4-4-0 calls at Teynham with a down Kent coast train in April 1959. It appears that most of the preparatory work for electrification was complete by this time. *G. R. Siviour*

Below right: A rather woebegone 'Scotch Arthur', No 30769 *Sir Balan*, approaches Faversham in July 1959 with a faint shadow of the former 'Kentish Belle'. Such a scene was typical of the last days of steam on the former LCDR main line. *G. R. Siviour*

Above: A nine-coach Easter 1959 excursion special for Sheerness-on-Sea presents no special challenge for an unusual choice of power. Maunsell 'Q' class 0-6-0 goods locomotive No 30545 built in 1939 steams through the orchard belt near Rainham. *G. R. Siviour*

Right: An exceptionally busy Sunday at Rainham on 12 September 1954. Class D No 31737 has arrived with a special train from Liverpool Street while 'R' class No 31671 is about to take the train on to Sheerness.

Below: Easter Monday 1959 was a busy day for excursion trains to the Kent coast, and the choice of locomotives for these duties could be quite eclectic. 'N' class 2-6-0 No 31400, although originally designated for freight, was equally at home on passenger duties as seen near Teynham. *G. R. Siviour*

Above: Faversham shed was well known as the home of interesting pre-Grouping relics which were usually employed on less-demanding duties on the Dover line. Wainwright 'D' class 4-4-0 No 31577 makes a characteristically dignified exit from Faversham on 28 December 1954 with an all-stations service for Dover Priory. This was a product of Ashford Works in 1906 and was withdrawn in 1956.

Right: The curved splashers of the 'L' class 4-4-0s gave them a particular grace. Here, No 31779, designed by Wainwright and built by Borsig of Berlin in 1913, waits outside Faversham station on 28 December 1954 with a three-coach 'birdcage' set before leaving as another local for Dover Priory.

Right: Faversham shed was located at the bifurcation of the routes to Ramsgate (left) and Dover (right). The long footbridge, left, gave access to the shed and the sidings which were connected to the Faversham Creek branch.

Left: 'King Arthur' class 4-6-0 No 30769 *Sir Balan* arrives at Whitstable & Tankerton station with a Ramsgate train on 18 April 1957. This replaced the original LCDR station of Whitstable Town in 1915. There is evidence of platform extension work associated with the forthcoming electrification.

Below: The coastline between Whitstable and Birchington has been vulnerable to erosion for many years, and in the spring of 1953 coastal defences were breached. The ensuing floods damaged the railway between Herne Bay and Birchington as well as near Seasalter. In response an emergency shuttle passenger service linked Faversham to Herne Bay powered by a Kirtley 'R' class 0-4-4T dating from 1891, with a two-coach push-pull set. No 31671, normally more at home on the Gravesend West branch, was a most unusual visitor to Whitstable during this period, as seen on 16 April 1953.

Left: Chestfield & Swalecliffe Halt was a rather unlovely pre-cast concrete structure assembled from a kit manufactured at the SR concrete works at Exmouth Junction in 1930, but it had a special significance for the author. 'King Arthur' class 4-6-0 No 30764 *Sir Gawain* makes a brief stop there with a Ramsgate–Victoria train in August 1951.

Right: The station at Herne Bay, inconveniently situated on the edge of town, presents a classic steam era scene as BR Standard Class 5 4-6-0 No 73082 saunters away with a lightweight Ramsgate–Victoria train on 17 April 1957. Electrification is not yet in evidence, the LCDR goods shed still handled an occasional vanload, and the water column and signalbox were still in use.

Below right: Another BR Standard Class 5 4-6-0, No 73086, is about to leave Herne Bay with a Victoria–Ramsgate train on the same day.

Above: Five years later the roller-coaster subsidence-prone concrete platforms at Chestfield & Swalecliffe Halt had been replaced by lighter weight wooden structures — a curious reversal from the norm for an ex-Southern station. 'King Arthur' 4-6-0 No 30767 *Sir Valence* leads a nine-coach formation *en route* to Ramsgate on 4 October 1956.

Right: 'R' class 0-4-4T No 31671 approaches Chestfield & Swalecliffe Halt with a Faversham–Herne Bay flood emergency shuttle service on 16 April 1953. Contrary to normal trends, the Thanet Way arterial road which paralleled the railway was subsequently downgraded and replaced by a new motorway following a different route. A Sainsbury's supermarket and a McDonald's restaurant have now transformed the rural landscape here.

Below: 'L1' 4-4-0 No 31782 omits a stop at Chestfield & Swalecliffe Halt with a Victoria–Ramsgate train in August 1953.

Above: An 'N' class 2-6-0 crosses Reculver Marshes with an up Kent coast train in August 1957. This section of the route may be increasingly vulnerable to encroachment by the North Sea as a result of global warming. *G. R. Siviour*

Below: Bulleid 'Battle of Britain' class 4-6-2 No 34086 *219 Squadron* approaches Birchington on 18 April 1957 with a Victoria–Ramsgate train that includes three Pullman cars.

Above right: BR Standard Class 5 4-6-0 No 73083 leaves Birchington on the same day with a Ramsgate–Victoria train. Between 1918 and 1925, the Manston Camp Light Railway provided passenger and goods service from a junction at Upper End Farm west of Birchington to the RAF aerodrome then under construction at Manston Camp.

Right: The tidy and unassuming LCDR station buildings which consisted of a cottage-style structure and a later annexe at Birchington, as seen on the author's visit on 18 April 1957.

Above: 'King Arthur' class 4-6-0 No 30794 *Sir Ector de Maris* pauses with a Victoria–Ramsgate train at Westgate-on-Sea. One of the now-vanished icons of every high street is visible on the right.

Below: The impressive and spacious SR station at Margate was built to handle the holiday crowds of another era. This was the view west towards Westgate on 27 September 1957.

Above right: Originally built as a 'D' class 4-4-0 at Ashford in 1902, No 31739 became a 'D1' after rebuilding in 1927, and lasted until 1961. Its capacity was not going to be over-taxed by this stopping train to Ashford via Canterbury West awaiting departure at Margate on 27 September 1957.

Right: As No 31739 pulls out of Margate with an Ashford train, also on 27 September 1957, we have a glimpse on the right of the site of the former SER terminus at Margate Sands.

Below right: Margate East, located ¾ mile east of the main station, was the most unassuming station to serve the resort and few trains stopped there. With two weeks of life remaining when photographed, it was nonetheless staffed until closure on 4 May 1953.

Top: Immaculate rebuilt 'West Country' 4-6-2 No 34017 *Ilfracombe* has only a few more miles to go as it leaves Broadstairs for Ramsgate on 10 April 1958.

Above: 'King Arthur' class 4-6-0 No 30766 *Sir Geraint* attracts fleeting attention from two trainspotters on 10 April 1958 during its brief stop at Dumpton Park with a Victoria–Ramsgate train.

Above: The station buildings at Dumpton Park dated from the 1926 rationalisation of rail lines on the Isle of Thanet in which the stations at Ramsgate Harbour, Ramsgate Town and Margate Sands were closed, together with the lines serving them, and a new line opened, connecting Broadstairs to modern stations at Dumpton Park and Ramsgate.
Notwithstanding its location within the urban community of Ramsgate, the station at Dumpton Park, seen here in April 1958, was subsequently reduced to the status of unstaffed halt and today only an island platform and canopy remain.

Left: The extensive station and yard at Ramsgate as seen from the southern end on 10 April 1958. The loco shed, water tower and coaling plant are visible to the left and a 'D1' 4-4-0 and a 'C' class 0-6-0 stand outside the carriage shed. In the right background can be seen the lofty but inconveniently situated station building erected by the Southern Railway in 1926 as part of the Thanet rail line rationalisation project.

Left: From the north end at Ramsgate, the station, carriage shed, locomotive servicing facilities and goods yard comprised a busy scene in April 1958, before electrification.

FAVERSHAM–DOVER

Above: Class U1 2-6-0 No 31890 trundles a trainload of pit props and coal empties destined for Snowdown Colliery and vans assigned to apple shipments from local orchards, past a row of oast houses and a backdrop of hop gardens midway between Faversham and Selling on 28 December 1954. Today, hop acreage is greatly reduced, and Kent has conceded the title of UK's leading hop-growing county to Herefordshire. Many oast houses have been converted to stylish country residences for weekenders, commuters and retirees. Selling was formerly an important loading point for fruit traffic, as was nearby Graveney siding on the Faversham–Whitstable section.

Below: In the 1950s, Canterbury's stations retained a strong sense of their pre-Grouping ownership. The cavernous depths of the train shed at Canterbury East reflected the practice of the LCDR of providing generous protection against the elements for patrons at some of its busier stations, although such a design was not proof against the biting winds of East Kent. Other examples were at one time to be found at Ramsgate Harbour and Dover, while that at Sittingbourne also survived until the Fifties. It is clear that initial preparations for electrification have begun at Canterbury East when visited on 27 September 1957 and a healthy volume of goods traffic is being handled by the goods yard to the south of the station.

Left: Local trains were leisurely affairs on the Dover section of the former LCDR as epitomised by Class 4 2-6-4T No 42076 and a rake of Maunsell corridor stock forming this Dover Priory–Faversham all-stations train on 27 September 1957. Conductor rails and pre-cast concrete platform extension components on the right await installation.

Left: A notable feature at Canterbury East is the elevated signalbox which was designed to give adequate visibility for the signalman over the station roof. In the Fifties, the box contained a lever frame installed by the SECR in 1911. Most of this equipment was replaced before 1983 and thereafter Canterbury East functioned as the principal intermediate box between Faversham and Shepherds Well. Photographed on 27 September 1957.

Below: Newly delivered 4-CEP EMU No 7140 pauses at Canterbury East on 23 May 1959 while on driver training duty. The platform canopies had been removed from the unopened station at Lullingstone and have replaced the overall roof, although few other station features changed here during electrification.

Right: The quiet country station at Bekesbourne was, with the exception of its SR lamp standards, quite a study in the Victorian villa style of LCDR architecture. In this September 1957 view towards Canterbury East, it is clear the local coal merchant was the mainstay of goods traffic that was subsequently withdrawn in 1961. In common with Selling, Adisham and Snowdown, the station has remained open although unstaffed in recent times.

Above: A grimy Fairburn Class 4 2-6-4T, No 42076, stops briefly at a deserted Bekesbourne station on 27 September 1957 with an all-stations Faversham–Dover Priory train. There have been recent suggestions that services at Bekesbourne be reduced to peak hours only.

Right: Set amidst the chalk downlands, Adisham station retained an authentic LCDR flavour prior to electrification as seen in this view towards Bekesbourne on 23 May 1959. The commodious goods facilities, which might easily inspire a modeller, were closed in 1962.

Above: A Dover Priory–Faversham train calls at Aylesham Halt on 23 May 1959. The prominent winding gear of Snowdown Colliery can be seen in the background, left. The mine was the principal employer of Aylesham residents.

Left: Aylesham, the largest community between Canterbury and Dover, was planned in the 1920s as a new town for miners employed at nearby Snowdown Colliery, which operated from 1912 to 1987. Initially there were proposals to accommodate a population of 15,000, but this target was not achieved and 4,000 was the limit of its growth. With electrification, passenger facilities at Aylesham were upgraded from halt to station status. Here, on 23 May 1959, an up train from Dover Priory to Faversham pauses in an urban landscape more reminiscent of the industrial Midlands.

Left: LCDR tranquillity at Shepherds Well. To the northwest the railway cuts through the chalk upland *en route* to Snowdown & Nonington Halt. Beyond the goods shed can be seen the junction with the connecting spur to the former East Kent Light Railway which had been reduced in status at this time (May 1959) to that of a spur serving Tilmanstone Colliery. The goods shed ceased to function in 1963.

Top: 'Battle of Britain' class No 34066 *Spitfire* resolutely tackles the hilly, former LCDR main line after emerging from 2,376-yard Shepherds Well Tunnel with a Dover Marine–Victoria boat express in 1960. The normal route for these services was via the former SER main line through Ashford and Tonbridge. *G. R. Siviour*

Above: Veteran 'O1' class 0-6-0 No 31065, originally designed by Stirling and rebuilt by Wainwright in 1908, has just coupled up to a brake van for another trip to Tilmanstone Colliery as Maunsell 'N' class 2-6-0 No 31817, of 1922 vintage, coasts through Shepherds Well with a down goods in August 1960. No 31065 was withdrawn in 1961 prior to a chequered period in preservation which happily culminated in it becoming the pride of the Bluebell Railway. *G. R. Siviour*

Left: 'Schools' class 4-4-0 No 30921 *Shrewsbury* makes a relatively rare appearance on a Dover Marine–Victoria boat train in August 1960, passing the site of Stonehall & Lydden Halt, which was closed on 5 April 1954. Nearby, a colliery was built which never functioned, although its yard was used as a servicing point for locomotives requisitioned by the military for use on the Elham Valley line and on local artillery trains during World War II. *G. R. Siviour*

Below: Wainwright 'D' class 4-4-0 No 31737 has just run around a special passenger train at Kearsney after traversing the rarely used Kearsney loop line on 12 September 1954.

Above: Another rare passenger movement over the Kearsney loop was that of 'O1' class 0-6-0 No 31258 with a Railway Enthusiasts' Club (REC) special train en route to Minster Junction on 23 May 1959 following a visit to the rump of the former East Kent Light Railway. The loop line did not have a significant role following electrification and was subsequently closed.

Below: 'Schools' class 4-4-0 No 30926 *Repton* emerges from Priory Tunnel before stopping at Dover with a Margate–Charing Cross train on 11 August 1953.

SER MAIN LINE

Above: Summertime at Hildenborough: Wainwright 'H' class 0-4-4T No 31184, built at Ashford in 1915, drifts in with a Tonbridge–Sevenoaks Tubs Hill local in August 1957. This locomotive was withdrawn a year later. *G. R. Siviour*

Right: After completing a spell of duty on the Westerham branch, 'H' class 0-4-4T No 31523 and empty stock has emerged from Sevenoaks tunnel and is about to pass Weald box *en route* to the shed at Tonbridge for servicing in April 1958. *G. R. Siviour*

Right: The 'Merchant Navy' Pacific leading the up 'Golden Arrow' in August 1958 leaves a blanket of smoke in its wake and takes the through road as it roars through Paddock Wood. *G. R. Siviour*

Top: Rebuilt 'West Country' No 34015 *Exmouth* takes the through road at Paddock Wood with the up 'Golden Arrow' in March 1961. The elevated signalbox straddles the up slow line. *G. R. Siviour*

Above: Class L1 4-4-0 No 31783 arrives at Paddock Wood on 31 August 1958 with a down stopping train. *G. R. Siviour*

Above: 'D1' 4-4-0 No 31735 takes the Maidstone West line at Paddock Wood with a hop-pickers' special on 31 August 1958. Stock forming another hop-pickers' special destined for Hawkhurst is stabled beside the distinctive raised signalbox, beyond which the regular Hawkhurst branch train occupies the bay platform. *G. R. Siviour*

Left: A departing Hawkhurst branch train on 31 August 1958 provides a vantage point to witness Wainwright 'C' class standard goods 0-6-0 No 31590, built at Ashford in 1908 and destined to last until 1962. It accelerates away from Paddock Wood with a down main line hop-pickers' special. The eclectic assortment of rolling stock typified these trains and includes a former SECR matchboard-sided second class corridor coach built for boat train service in 1921. *G. R. Siviour*

Left: Wealden flyer: 'D1' 4-4-0 No 31739 makes light work of the Ramsgate portion of the 7.24am Cannon Street–Ramsgate train on the raceway near Marden in July 1960. This train divided at Tonbridge, with the rear portion serving the Maidstone West line while the Ramsgate section covered the 29¾ miles to Ashford in 29 minutes without stops. *G. R. Siviour*

Left: 'Battle of Britain' class 4-6-2 No 34070 *Manston* ambles through the orchards near Marden in June 1961 with a down stopping train. *G. R. Siviour*

Below left: 'N' class Mogul No 31862 is seen in the busy erecting shop at Ashford Works during an enthusiasts' visit in 1961. *G. R. Siviour*

Right: Steam reigned supreme at Ashford shed in 1953. Stroudley 'Terrier' No 32678, a visitor from Rolvenden shed on the Kent & East Sussex line, shares this crowded scene on 25 May 1953 with 'D' class 4-4-0 No 31734 and 'N1' class 2-6-0 No 31870.

Right: Veteran 'D' class 4-4-0 No 31734 awaits the call at Ashford shed on 25 May 1953; grimy but still handsome, it was built by Sharp, Stewart in 1901 to a Wainwright design. In the early Fifties, the 'Ds' were assigned to lighter duties and in 1953, 18 of the original 51 members of the class survived. The last of them were withdrawn in 1956, with No 31737 becoming one of the treasures of the National Collection and going on display at the Museum of British Transport, Clapham, before being transferred to the National Railway Museum at York.

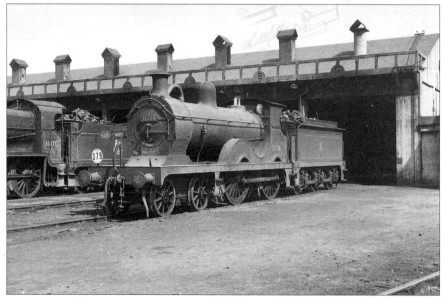

Below: The typical SER staggered platforms of Smeeth station seldom echoed to the footsteps of passengers so it came as no surprise when closure occurred on 4 January 1954, just a few days after this photograph was taken on 31 December.

Above: While passengers had largely deserted Smeeth station, goods traffic in the sidings to the east lingered for a few more years. This scene, on 31 December 1953 is scarcely recognisable today.

Below: 'R1' class 0-6-0T No 31154 gingerly eases a Victoria–Folkestone Harbour boat train down the incline from Folkestone Junction on 16 August 1953. The 'R1s' were originally a Stirling design of 1894, but were rebuilt by Wainwright, this locomotive going through the works in 1912. It was to remain at the small subshed at Folkestone Junction for two more years after this photograph was taken, before withdrawal.

Above: A trio of 'R1' tanks, Nos 31137, 31178 and 31154, start the 1-in-30 climb from Folkestone Harbour to Folkestone Junction with a boat train bound for Victoria on 16 August 1953. The spectacle of such elderly steam power hard at work was always a joy to the eyes and music to the ears.

Left: A 'Schools' class 4-4-0 hurries through Folkestone Warren with a London train. This scenic section of line is characterised by geological instability and is scarred by earlier and unsuccessful attempts to build a tunnel under the English Channel.

Below: This was one of the last occasions when the 'Golden Arrow' was worked by steam, with Bulleid 'West Country' Pacific No 34100 *Appledore* slowing through Folkestone Warren as it nears the end of its journey to Dover Marine in 1961. *G. R. Siviour*

Right: Against a backdrop of Dover harbour and the legendary white cliffs, BR Standard 2-6-4 tank approaches Abbotscliff Tunnel with an up local train. *G. R. Siviour*

REDHILL–TONBRIDGE

Above: 'C' class 0-6-0 No 31716 plods through pouring rain near Penshurst with a Tonbridge–Redhill goods in June 1957. *G. R. Siviour*

SITTINGBOURNE– SHEERNESS-ON-SEA BRANCH

Right: Double-heading on the Sheerness branch. This Sheerness train, pausing at Queenborough on 7 June 1954, presented an interesting contrast between old and new. Motive power consisted of two Ivatt Class 2 2-6-2Ts, Nos 41311 and 41312, which were allocated to Gillingham shed, while the passenger accommodation was provided by a pair of three-coach 'birdcage' sets of SECR vintage. Four years had elapsed since the demise of the Sheppey Light Railway and the former branch platform on the left was now bereft of track. In recent years, the Sheerness branch has attracted attention as one of the early community rail partnerships in Kent.

Right: Half a century has brought many changes to isolated and windswept Swale Halt. On 7 June 1954, Ivatt Class 2 2-6-2T No 41311 has just crossed the Kingsferry Bridge, the second in a series of lift bridges that have connected the Isle of Sheppey to the mainland. The train is destined to stop at the rickety wooden platform which began life as a staff halt in 1913. It was subsequently replaced by a pre-cast concrete structure when the line was electrified and a new and massive lift bridge was built after its predecessor was severely damaged when struck by a vessel. The traffic is waiting for the lights to change before gaining access to the combined rail and road link. Much has changed here since: the Maidstone & District coach is history and the road was relocated to connect to the third bridge. In 2006, the opening of a new (fourth) high-level fixed road bridge resulted in the final separation of road and rail access to Sheppey and the removal of a highway bottleneck. Meanwhile it is surprising that Swale Halt survives, although only a few workers at nearby Ridham Dock make use of it.

Right: The second lift bridge at Swale, as seen from a special train from Liverpool Street via the East London line and Blackheath *en route* to Sheerness 12 September 1954. The locomotive was (for the photographer) the seemingly inevitable 'R' class 0-4-4T No 31671.

THE HUNDRED OF HOO BRANCH

Left: The railways of Kent could never be accused of failing to exploit opportunities to develop holiday traffic, but there were failures. By comparison with the featureless windswept marshland where optimistic promoters sought to establish Allhallows-on-Sea as a residential development and seaside resort, even the Leysdown terminus of the Sheppey Light Railway could be described as scenic. At Allhallows the Southern Railway station and adjacent hotel, seen here on 3 September 1954, were expressions of an unfulfilled dream. The short branch, which joined the Port Victoria line at Stoke Junction Halt, lasted for only 29 years.

Below: The author recalls a sense of bewilderment on alighting for the first time at Allhallows-on-Sea where there seemed to be virtually no settlement. Perhaps 'H' class No 31193 had, on this occasion in 1960, delivered a few hardy caravanners intent on getting away from it all on the marshes. *G. R. Siviour*

Left: One of the more obscure passenger services operated by the Southern Region in the 1950s served the Isle of Grain at the convergence of the estuaries of the Thames and Medway. 'H' class 0-4-4T No 31518 waits at the unsheltered island platform at Grain with one of the two daily passenger trains to Gravesend Central on 3 September 1954. Ostensibly a workmens' service for the BP oil refinery, passenger business was minimal and the station was closed within ten years.

Left: When the BP oil refinery was built between 1948 and 1952, the original rail route to the former ferry terminal at Port Victoria, where two successive stations had occupied lonely positions in the marshes between 1882 and 1951, was obliterated by industrial development. After closure of the station to passengers on 2 December 1961 the refinery operated until 1982, when the site was occupied by new industries including the Thamesport container terminal, an oil-fired power station, a liquefied natural gas import terminal and, for a brief period of intense activity, the plant which fabricated segments for the Channel Tunnel lining. As seen here on 3 September 1954, the generous proportions of the island passenger platform were, with the exception of a few ceremonial occasions, absurdly excessive for the two-coach push-pull trains that provided the service. However, the expansion of industrial and port activity on the Isle of Grain has assured the survival of the branch from Hoo Junction as an important route for goods traffic — a relative rarity in Kent.

Right: Southern pre-cast concrete did nothing to ameliorate the desolation of the treeless marshland at Stoke Junction Halt where 'H' class No 31518 pauses with a Gravesend train on 3 September 1954. Unexpected activity at this isolated spot was nevertheless provided by the local coal merchant seen here in the midst of a time-honoured rail-to-road transfer process.

Top: It is unlikely that local farms generated much passenger business at isolated Middle Stoke Halt where 'H' class No 31518 makes a brief stop with an Allhallows–Gravesend train on the same day.

Above: Double-heading on the Hundred of Hoo. The passing loop at Sharnal Street station is occupied by an Allhallows-on-Sea train hauled by two 'H' class tanks, Nos 31263 and 31193. This was an interchange point with the Chattenden Naval Tramway which closed in 1940 and the Kingsnorth Light Railway which ceased operations during the 1940s, having served the bitumen plant of Berry Wiggins & Co. *G. R. Siviour*

THE WESTERHAM BRANCH

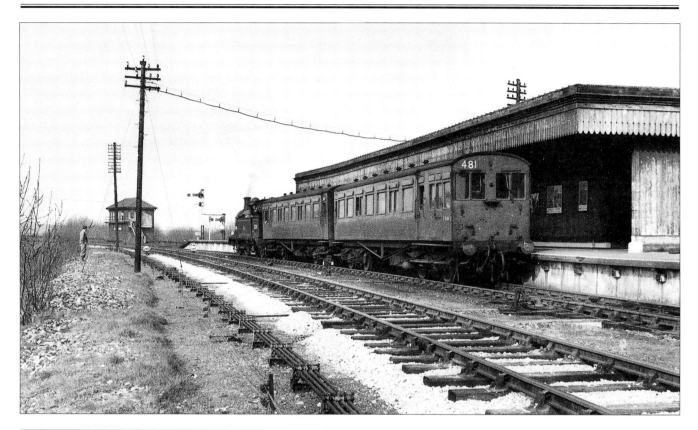

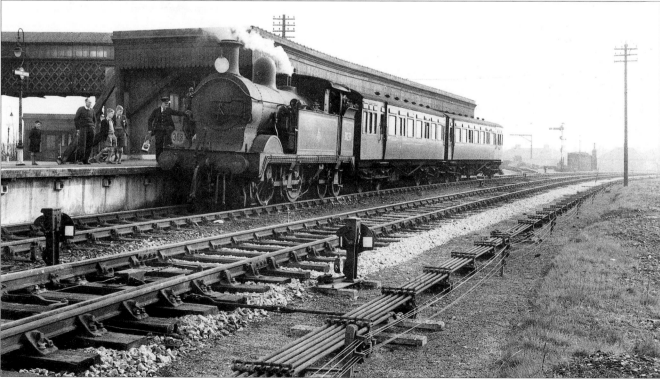

Top: The Westerham branch push-pull train awaits departure at the branch platform at Dunton Green in February 1956, behind 'H' class 0-4-4T No 31239.

Above: The guard is about to affix an oil lamp to No 31239 before it propels the branch train out of Dunton Green. Since closure and the obliteration of most of the Westerham branch by the construction of the M25 motorway, the junction station has been demoted to unstaffed status.

Above: 'H' class No 31263 propels a train from Westerham in August 1959 as it approaches the junction at Dunton Green. *G. R. Siviour*

Left: A Westerham train enters Chevening Halt in February 1956. This site is now unrecognisable as it is covered by a junction of the M25 motorway.

Left: No 31239 approaches Chevening Halt with a train for Dunton Green in February 1956.

Above: No 31177 propels the Westerham train into the peaceful country station at Brasted on 26 June 1953.

Left: A summer's day at the typical SER clapboard station of Brasted, looking towards Chevening Halt, again on 26 June 1953. The station building finally lingered as a battered hulk while motorway construction proceeded where the track once lay.

Left: An idyllic rural scene where the motorway now dominates. No 31177 propels the Westerham branch train near Park Farm, west of Brasted. *G. R. Siviour*

Below left: A ubiquitous 'H' class tank propels the branch train against a backdrop of the North Downs, three quarters of a mile east of Westerham in April 1958. This peaceful scene has been irretrievably transformed by the traffic-choked M25 which now covers the old railway right of way. *G. R. Siviour*

Above: The SER atmosphere at Westerham, depicted on 26 June 1953, lasted until the end, replete with a station of traditional design, wooden goods shed, and loco watering facilities. The loco shed had been removed at an earlier date.

Below: The crew has a tea break at Westerham before returning with No 31177 on another trip to the junction at Dunton Green on 26 June 1953.

ASHFORD–MINSTER VIA CANTERBURY WEST

Left: Fairburn 2-6-4T No 42070 is near Chilham on a Margate–Ashford stopping train on 10 August 1953. The absence of discs on the locomotive is unusual.

Below: The peace of a summer's evening in 1961 near Chartham is hardly disturbed by the passage of a Ramsgate–Ashford local train hauled by 'N' class Mogul No 31413 in August 1961. *G. R. Siviour*

Top: 'N' class 2-6-0 No 31875 approaches Canterbury West with an eight-coach 'birdcage' set and utility van on a Margate–Ashford service, 10 August 1953.

Above: Class 4 2-6-4Ts were making their presence felt in Kent during the early Fifties on duties such this Ramsgate–Ashford via Canterbury West train seen approaching Minster Junction on 13 August 1953 headed by No 42070. The original spur to the Sandwich line is in the foreground, and the contrast between the locomotive and the SECR rolling stock forming the train is noticeable.

Right: The northern section of the former SER Ramsgate Town–Margate Sands direct line, which was closed in 1926, was retained in the Fifties for shunting movements via a connection to the former LCDR east of Margate station. The line extended to the southern limits of Margate suburbia as seen in this view dated 27 September 1957.

CANTERBURY & WHITSTABLE BRANCH

Right: The north portal of Tyler Hill Tunnel on 19 April 1953. The oldest railway tunnel in the county (built in 1830) was so narrow that only certain 'R1' class locomotives with cut-down cabs and shortened chimneys could negotiate it. Trains destined for Whitstable Harbour faced a continuous uphill gradient of 1:56 all the way from the junction at Canterbury West to the site of Blean and Tyler Hill Halt. This included the half-mile transit of the tunnel which could threaten both loco crew and guard with asphyxiation and a bombardment by hot cinders, and even a walk through the tunnel could induce claustrophobia. The tunnel is now blocked by debris after the roof collapsed and it is no longer passable, the land above having now been incorporated into the campus of the University of Kent.

Right: Railway photography for the author began, most appropriately, on the oldest section of the Southern with a Brownie box camera in August 1951. The extremely tight clearance imposed by Tyler Hill Tunnel is obvious as Stirling 'R1' class 0-6-0T No 31339 with its cut-down cab emerges from the north portal with the daily Whitstable Harbour goods. It would take five minutes or so before the ensuing build-up of smoke ceased to pour from the tunnel mouth. The portal is now bricked up.

Below: The only remnant of the three halts on the 'Crab and Winkle' line in August 1951 was the shelter and vestige of the platform at South Street. At the nearby level crossing stood the Halt Stores and to the north can be seen the 1934 art deco-style bridge that carried the Thanet Way.

Above: 'R1' No 31010 approaches the Thanet Way bridge south of Whitstable on 15 August 1952, with a return goods for Canterbury conveying coal empties and grain. This is close to the site of the winding engine that hauled trains up the incline out of Whitstable between 1832 and 1846.

Below: There was nothing posed about this August 1951 scene in which 'R1' No 31010 crossed the former LCDR main line with the daily goods from Canterbury West as a 'Battle of Britain' Pacific left Whitstable & Tankerton with a Victoria–Ramsgate train. The happy coincidence is further enhanced by a glimpse, on the right, of the oldest railway bridge in Kent, which sadly, was sacrificed later, on the altar of road improvement.

Above: Having completed shunting duties at Whitstable Harbour, No 31010 sets out on its return trip to Canterbury with a light load. It is passing the third station to be built on the line, which was named Whitstable Town by the SER in 1894. It was closed to passengers in 1931, but part of the station building was visible on the left on 12 August 1952. The tarmacadam plant, a notable rail user and feature of the harbour, was destined to expand, prosper and outlive the railway.

Right: 'R1' No 31339 shunts at Whitstable Harbour in August 1951. Incoming waterborne grain traffic destined for forwarding by rail to Ashford is much in evidence. In the absence of the daily goods train, horses were used in the harbour sidings as the wagon turntables on the west and north quays could not accommodate locomotives.

Right: Following the lifting of track at Whitstable Harbour, the second station, opened by the SER in 1846, still survived. Beyond the site of the level crossing at Tankerton Road, the third station, opened in 1894, was also still extant until development largely obliterated the site.

FARNINGHAM ROAD–GRAVESEND WEST BRANCH

Above: The wayside station of Farningham Road (for Sutton-at-Hone) on the former LCDR main line was the junction for the little-known branch line to Gravesend West Street. Only the presence of the third rail was at odds with the South Eastern & Chatham atmosphere as 'R' class 0-4-4T No 31671 leaves with an infrequent push-pull train for Gravesend. The locale is less rural now due to the expansion of housing for London commuters and the massive warehouse operated by Corus Steel that occupies the site of the former goods yard at the east end of the station. This view, like the others showing this branch, was taken on 1 August 1953.

Above: A Farningham Road–Gravesend West Street train propelled by No 31671 stops briefly at Longfield Halt. The line was double track through to Gravesend West.

Left: Longfield Halt was inconveniently located for the village and was situated in a deep chalk cutting subject to rockfalls. A typical wooden SECR railmotor halt, it was opened in 1913 and lasted for 40 years until closure. In 1953, it was unimaginable that this quiet branch was ultimately destined to form a section of the Channel Tunnel Rail Link.

Left: No 31671 propels a Gravesend West Street train through the chalk cutting towards Southfleet after leaving Longfield Halt.

Below left: Southfleet, like its closed neighbour Rosherville, consisted of an island platform. Its yard continued to handle goods traffic until 1968. Now the scene has been totally changed and is rural no longer, with much of the old alignment filled in and redeveloped for housing. Northeast of the station site Stage 2 of the Channel Tunnel Rail Link now dominates the scene, while to the south, the remaining and upgraded section of the branch joins the recently built high-speed route to the coast via a curved connection.

Above: Southfleet station from the east. A curious feature of the branch was that although it provided a route for electricity cables linking the Central Electricity Generating Board plant at Northfleet to the substation on the electrified main line at Fawkham, the branch itself was never a candidate for electrification. The channel conveying these cables was a prominent feature at Southfleet. This essentially rural scene was completed by a row of railway cottages and the stationmaster's house.

Left: The site of the yard and signalbox at Southfleet has been transformed by Stage 2 of the CTRL route to St Pancras which now crosses here.

Below: No 31671 approaches Rosherville with a train from Farningham Road.

Above: A remarkable survival in 1953 was Rosherville station which had been closed for 20 years. Opened in 1886, the station served the popular Rosherville botanical gardens which had been created in 1839, the 17-acre site occupying a former chalk pit. Ironically, as the rail network expanded, the gardens declined and they closed in 1910. Nevertheless, the station remained staffed until 1928 and continued as an unstaffed halt for a further five years. Thereafter, the abandoned weed-grown island platform survived until demolition.

Below: Gravesend West, where the dilapidated station buildings were located in a 'V' formed by the platforms, had clearly seen better days. It is interesting to note that Gravesend was also connected by ferry to Tilbury Riverside, which was also destined to lose its passenger rail service. Attached to the station by a covered walkway was an embarkation point for steamer services to Rotterdam which were linked to London, Victoria, by very modest boat trains during the 1920s and '30s. West Street pier also had a long history of steamer connections to Southend, Clacton, Walton-on-the-Naze and Felixstowe.

Above: Gravesend West remained a fairly busy terminal for goods traffic. 'C' class 0-6-0 No 31722 from Bricklayers Arms shed shunts the yard near the weatherworn signalbox.

Left: On the last day of passenger service, 1 August 1953, 'R' class No 31671, one of a class that had seen many years of service on the branch, was assigned to perform the last rites. Here, it takes water before an afternoon trip to Farningham Road.

Below: Such was the forgotten nature of the line that the additional coaches provided for the last train from Gravesend West were scarcely necessary. A somewhat grimy No 31671 performed the honours.

SANDLING JUNCTION–HYTHE BRANCH

Right: In 1951, the Hythe (Kent) branch was something of an anomaly. The service frequency was minimal, Newmans bus service had captured the passenger business, the few trains that ran were usually empty, and the station at Hythe was poorly located. Here, 'R' class 0-4-4T No 31671 leaves the branch platform at Sandling Junction with a two-coach train for the 1½-mile trip to Hythe in August 1951.

Right: No 31671 simmers quietly amongst the weeds at the decayed SER station at Hythe in August 1951. The obscure hillside location of the station on the edge of town and vestigial service had condemned the line to oblivion and, inevitably, closure came on 3 December 1951 when even the last train attracted little attention.

Below: The forgotten nature of the Hythe branch was epitomised by the degree to which the classic SER station building at Hythe was falling victim to encroaching vegetation.

Below right: The arrival of the 1.30pm Saturdays-only train has brought five passengers to Hythe on this August day in 1951. The loop remains as a reminder of its former role as intermediate station on the abandoned line to Sandgate, which closed in 1931. No 31671 was subsequently to become one of the author's most frequently photographed locomotives as it migrated from one backwater to another in Kent.

KENT & EAST SUSSEX LIGHT RAILWAY

Above: Long before the Kent & East Sussex line from Headcorn to Robertsbridge attracted widespread attention and preservation efforts were launched, this delightful backwater was the object of regular pilgrimages by the devotees of Colonel Stephens and all his works. It was particularly worthwhile to leave London at an early hour on Monday mornings in order to witness the double-headed first departure from Headcorn. The apparently excessive motive power was attributable to the need to reposition locomotives that had been serviced at Ashford over the weekend. On this occasion, on 2 November 1953, venerable Stirling 'O1' class 0-6-0 No 31065 and sprightly Stroudley 'Terrier' 0-6-0T No 32659 were about to begin another 'arduous' week of work based on Rolvenden shed.

Below: On other days, the first morning departure from Headcorn was entrusted to a solitary 'O1'. It is interesting to note, in this August 1951 view, the ratio of railway staff to passengers on the KESR platform at Headcorn prior to the departure of No 31370 for the 9½-mile run to Rolvenden in a time of 65 minutes. An additional hour or so would deliver the true connoisseur to Robertsbridge after a loco change at Rolvenden.

Left: At a distance of over two miles from the village it purported to serve, the condition of the station at Frittenden Road suggests that few travellers were fooled by the station's name. Insertion of a few token concrete sleepers did not extend far in the direction of Headcorn. This was the scene on 25 May 1953.

Below left: Biddenden was the principal intermediate station and only passing loop between Headcorn and Tenterden Town. The relatively tidy condition of the premises on 25 May 1953 confirms the presence of station staff. With luck, the traveller could enjoy watching the thrills of fly shunting here during a 67-minute journey on the 3.15pm mixed train from Rolvenden to Headcorn.

Above: The economical provision of facilities on a light railway was evident in the signalling arrangements as well as level crossing protection at High Halden Road, on the same day as the previous view. The author vividly recalls a close encounter here between the hand pump trolley on which he was travelling and a Maidstone & District double-deck bus in August 1955 when the line was being dismantled. The look of astonishment on the bus driver's face will never be forgotten, and the whole episode could have been entitled 'Buster Keaton in the garden of England'.

Left: At the decidedly rickety Tenterden St Michael's Halt, seen here on 2 January 1954, the line curved northwards before entering a rare feature for a light railway — a short tunnel.

Below: 'O1' No 31370 rounds the curve into Tenterden Town with a morning train from Headcorn on 25 May 1953.

Above: 'O1' No 31065 coasts down the bank between Tenterden Town and Rolvenden with a train from Headcorn whose capacity has been increased by 100 per cent on 2 January 1954, the last day of traffic on the northern section of the line.

Left: Rolvenden was always the operating hub of the Kent & East Sussex. The locomotive shed, once the home of a virtual operating museum in the days of Colonel Stephens, is the building on the right. In the distance, No 31370 is shunting vans before returning to Headcorn with the 3.15pm mixed train in August 1951.

Below: Class O1 No 31370 is coaled at Rolvenden shed, which it shares with a 'Terrier' tank on January 1951.

Above left: A period of relative bustle occurs at Tenterden Town a few minutes later, following the arrival of No 31370 and its one-coach train from Headcorn. Preservation has brought many changes to this scene.

Left: The 3.15pm Rolvenden–Headcorn train hauled by No 31370 running tender-first pauses at Tenterden Town in August 1951, for the benefit of the photographer and a fond farewell by the only other passenger.

Right: It is train time at Rolvenden on 25 May 1953 and the gentleman with the purposeful stride, who has just arrived from Headcorn, is none other than the late John L. Smith, the well-known proprietor of Lens of Sutton, the transport bookshop.

Right: 'Terrier' No 32678 leaves Wittersham Road with the 12.20pm Robertsbridge–Tenterden Town mixed train on 28 November 1953. It is unlikely that the photographer then imagined that he would be manning the signalbox at Tenterden almost fifty years later. *G. R. Siviour*

Below: The high-pitched whistle of 'Terrier' tank No 32655 echoes across the water meadows of the Rother near Northiam close to the Kent border, as a trainload of enthusiasts arrives from Robertsbridge on 2 January 1954 on what then seemed would be the last day of passenger services on this line.

EAST KENT LIGHT RAILWAY

Top: The terminus of the former East Kent Light Railway at Shepherds Well survived and the yard continued to handle Tilmanstone coal traffic. Its reincarnation as a heritage railway centre was an unlikely prospect at that time, when visited on 11 August 1953. In the left background can be seen the connecting spur to the main line.

Above: Approaching the west portal of Golgotha Tunnel on 23 May 1959, with an REC special passenger train for Tilmanstone Colliery, is 'O1' 0-6-0 No 31258.

Right: Another 'O1', No 31434, has just emerged from the east portal of Golgotha Tunnel with a trainload of coal empties for Tilmanstone Colliery on 11 August 1953.

Below: Before preservation this was possibly the last passenger train from Shepherds Well to Eythorne, on 23 May 1959. No 31258 is about to stop to permit an enthusiast group to inspect the forlorn station building at Eythorne prior to traversing the remaining section of the former EKR to Tilmanstone Colliery.

Right: Double-headed 'O1s' Nos 31430 and 31434 make a fine sight as they approach Eythorne on 11 August 1953 with a trainload of coal from Tilmanstone. It is odd to reflect that the prominent landmark represented on the horizon by the colliery has now totally vanished.

Right: In 1953, the former main line of the East Kent Light Railway to Wingham had been lifted just beyond the junction with the Tilmanstone Colliery spur at Eythorne, as seen in this August view.

Below: The smallest of the collieries of the East Kent coalfield, Tilmanstone, operated from 1913 until 1987. All vestiges of the colliery have disappeared and the site is now an industrial estate. No 31258 returns to Shepherds Well with an enthusiasts' special on 23 May 1959.

MAIDSTONE EAST–ASHFORD

Left: Ramblers' specials were also popular among railway enthusiasts because of their unusual routeings and destinations. A spotless 'Battle of Britain' Pacific, No 34071 *601 Squadron*, has just arrived at Lenham on 19 April 1953 with a load of eager ramblers who are about to be disgorged upon the unsuspecting Kent countryside. The train originated at Victoria and travelled via Crystal Palace Low Level, Beckenham Junction, Swanley and Otford.

MEDWAY VALLEY LINE

Below: As a county, Kent was not notable for the architectural splendour of its stations, although the Victorian 'Tudor'-style building at Aylesford on the Medway Valley line north of Maidstone West is an interesting example of the use of ragstone rubble and Caen stone dressings. Photographed on 7 April 1956.

Bottom: The principal SER station at the county town of Kent was Maidstone West. The advent of World War II in 1939 cut short the prospect of extension of third-rail electrification south to Paddock Wood, with the result that the station remained an interchange between electric and steam traction for a further 22 years. A pair of 2-HAL units occupy the main down platform on 7 April 1956 after arriving from Charing Cross via Strood, where the train had divided, with an additional two 2-HALs being routed to another electrification railhead at Gillingham. The Medway Valley line had a distinctly split personality, serving a more industrialised landscape north of Maidstone, while the southern section to Paddock Wood was, and remains, quite rural in character. 'H' class 0-4-4T No 31193 waits in the bay platform with a push-pull train for Tonbridge.

Above: Wateringbury station, dating from shortly after the opening of the line in 1844, is like its near neighbour at Aylesford, a pleasing example of Victorian 'Tudor' style, although brick rather than stone is the building material. The addition of two vans to this Tonbridge–Maidstone West train on this occasion, on 31 August 1958, resulted in 'H' class tank No 31239 running bunker-first instead of in push-pull mode. It is regrettable that both Wateringbury and Aylesford are now unstaffed, which renders their buildings vulnerable. *G. R. Siviour*

Below: 'N' class 2-6-0 No 31860 threads the upper Medway Valley north of Wateringbury with a freight destined for Hoo Junction yard on 31 August 1958. *G. R. Siviour*

Right: Never beauty contest contenders, the Bulleid 'Q1' utility 0-6-0s were the epitome of naked power. The same day as the two previous views, No 33029 makes slow but steady progress with a Tonbridge–Hoo Junction freight south of Wateringbury. *G. R. Siviour*

Right: Beltring & Branbridges Halt is one of the few surviving sleeper-built railmotor halts of the SECR and dates from 1909. It escaped conversion to pre-cast concrete uniformity by the Southern and is at least a 20-minute walk from the two communities for which it is named. Its survival is surprising as Teston Crossing, a similar halt situated between Wateringbury and East Farleigh, was closed in 1959. Following automation of level crossing protection, the crossing keeper's cabin was surplus to requirements and the station, now known simply as Beltring, is no longer staffed. Another casualty at that time was the lamp room as illumination henceforth was by electricity instead of oil. In the right foreground in this 7 April 1956 view there is a glimpse of the short goods siding which handled farm produce until its removal in 1961.

Right: Nestling amongst the orchards, the tranquillity of Beltring & Branbridges Halt is briefly disturbed by the arrival of a push-pull service from Maidstone West to Tonbridge on 7 April 1956. The crossing keeper's cabin, right, bears the name Beltring Crossing, and the presence of a solitary wagon on the siding indicates the survival of occasional goods traffic.

PADDOCK WOOD–HAWKHURST BRANCH

Above: Goudhurst station, like Cranbrook, was notable for the contrast in accommodation provided for the stationmaster and passengers as seen in this June 1959 view northwards to Horsmonden.

Left: Wainwright 'C' class 0-6-0 No 31293 is about to depart from Cranbrook in September 1959 with the last full-length hop-pickers' train from Hawkhurst to London Bridge. *G. R. Siviour*

Left: 'H' class 0-4-4 tanks were regular performers on the Hawkhurst branch during the years before closure in 1961. No 31523 leaves Cranbrook with the branch train from Paddock Wood in September 1959. *G. R. Siviour*

Above: 'C' class 0-6-0 No 31716 approaches Cranbrook on its return trip from Hawkhurst with a single empty wagon and brake van in August 1958. *G. R. Siviour*

Left: The train crew is preparing to leave Hawkhurst on 6 August 1956 with 'H' class No 31239 on the return trip to Paddock Wood.

Below: The early association of the Hawkhurst branch with Colonel Holman Stephens is reflected in the design of the corrugated iron station building at the terminus. The signal cabin is dwarfed by the lofty water tower behind which can be seen the former locomotive shed which had not functioned as such since 1931. This view is also dated 6 August 1956.

Above left: Against a typical Wealden backdrop of hop gardens and oast houses, 'H' class tank No 31177 heads towards Hawkhurst near Pattenden Siding with the branch train in September 1958. *G. R. Siviour*

Left: The Hawkhurst was the very quintessence of a Kentish branch line. No 31177 is tackling the grade up to Cranbrook on a summer's day in August 1958. *G. R. Siviour*

TUNBRIDGE WELLS

Right: Built to a Wainwright design by Borsig of Berlin in 1914, 'L' class 4-4-0 No 31777 is not likely to be unduly taxed by the weight of a three-coach SECR 'birdcage' set forming a Sevenoaks–Brighton via Groombridge and Uckfield train at Tunbridge Wells Central on 16 April 1957. Cross-country journeys such as this are now but a distant memory.

Below: Maunsell 'Schools' class 4-4-0s were regular performers on the Hastings line, and Tunbridge Wells Central echoes to the clank of the coupling rods of No 30924 *Haileybury* as it continues on its way south with a Charing Cross–Hastings working on the same day.

Right: The former LBSCR station at Tunbridge Wells West was more impressive than the ex-SER Central station. In the Fifties, West station was busy with services on five routes to destinations in Sussex, Kent and London. A 2-6-4T has just arrived with a train from Victoria via the Oxted line; 16 April 1957.

Right: 'D1' 4-4-0 No 31489 radiates a certain Southern serenity as it approaches Tunbridge Wells West with a Sevenoaks–Brighton via Uckfield train on 2 November 1953.

Right: The new order makes its appearance as brand-new diesel-electric multiple-unit No 1002 adds to the decibel level at Tunbridge Wells Central before setting out on a driver-training run down the Hastings line, also on 16 April 1957. The width limitations imposed by the tunnels along the route are a striking feature of the front-end design.

Top: The undemanding cross-country Brighton–Sevenoaks turn was a frequent duty for 'D1' 4-4-0s, and No 31470 of Tonbridge shed pauses on 2 November 1953 while *en route* at Tunbridge Wells West.

Above: 'M7' class 0-4-4Ts were not traditional power at Tunbridge Wells West, but during their later days some members of the class were transferred from the Western section of the Southern Region to power the push-pull shuttle service to Oxted. The photographer was particularly pleased to encounter No 30054 on this duty on 16 April 1957 as it took on water at Tunbridge Wells West, having become familiar with this locomotive in previous haunts, such as the Meon Valley, Gosport and Borden branches.

GONE BUT NOT FORGOTTEN

Right: The Elham Valley line extended from Harbledown Junction Canterbury to Cheriton Junction near Shorncliffe. Regrettably its fine scenery was not matched by its contribution to net revenue, and passenger services were withdrawn in 1940. During World War II it achieved a strategic significance as a military railway providing rail-mounted long-range gun capability. The military continued to operate a goods service, but with the cessation of hostilities goods trains were withdrawn in September 1947. The two platforms that remained at Bridge in this August 1951 view towards Canterbury South reflected the double track that existed until singling in 1931. In later years, Bridge produced less revenue from passengers than any other station on the line.

Right: The most southerly station on the Elham Valley line at Lyminge witnessed a short-lived revival of passenger service to Shorncliffe in 1947. Six years later, on 12 August 1953, the abandoned trackbed extended northwards towards Elham while the station building continued in use as a residence.

Below: The remains of Sheerness East, the third and least significant station to serve the former dockyard town, looking towards Queenborough on 7 June 1954. The Sheppey Light Railway was dismantled during the summer of 1951, six months after the line was abandoned. For a while the roadbed made an excellent footpath all the way to Leysdown, as seen in this view dated 7 June 1954.

Above: At Eastchurch, the platform and crossing keeper's house remained after abandonment of the Sheppey Light Railway, although the barely noticeable earthworks along the old right of way, seen on 7 June 1954, suggested how soon most vestiges of the line would fade into oblivion.

Left: Further evidence that abandoned light railways were transitory features of the landscape was to be seen in April 1953 at Wingham Colliery Halt on the former East Kent Light Railway route to Canterbury Road, Wingham, where nature was rapidly reclaiming the site within five years of abandonment.

CHATTENDEN & UPNOR RAILWAY

Right: The Admiralty's Chattenden & Upnor Railway 0-4-2T No 49 *Burnett Hall* stands out of use at Chattenden Depot Yard on 7 April 1956. This 2ft 6in gauge locomotive was built by the Avonside Engine Company (No 2070) in 1933, spent its life on the C&UR, and was scrapped in 1956.

Right: A special passenger train on the C&UR at Church Crossing on 7 April 1956 headed by *Yard No 107* (Baguley/Drewry 2263) an 0-6-0 diesel mechanical built in 1949. In 1960, it was transferred to RNAD Ernesettle, Devon, and later moved to Broughton Moor, Cumberland, before passing to the Welshpool & Llanfair Light Railway where it rejoined ex-C&UR passenger rolling stock.

FAREWELL TO STEAM

Left: Rebuilt 'West Country' 4-6-2 No 34001 *Exeter* climbs away from London, Victoria, with the last steam service for Ramsgate on 14 June 1959. *G. R. Siviour*